TABLE O

INTRODUCTION 2

CHAPTER 1: CHILDHOOD, EARLY LIFE, AND HIGH SCHOOL CAREER 7

CHAPTER 2: COLLEGE CAREER 10

CHAPTER 3: NBA CAREER 14

CHAPTER 4: INTERNATIONAL CAREER 69

CHAPTER 5: PERSONAL LIFE 70

CHAPTER 6: IMPACT, LEGACY, AND FUTURE 71

MORE INFORMATION 74

REFERENCES 79

Introduction

Alfred Joel Horford Reynoso (born June 3, 1986) is a Dominican professional basketball player for the Oklahoma City Thunder of the National Basketball Association (NBA). Horford is a five-time NBA All-Star and is the highest paid Latin American basketball player. He also represents the Dominican Republic national team.

He played college basketball for the Florida Gators and was the starting centre on their back-to-back National Collegiate Athletic Association (NCAA) national championships teams in 2006 and 2007. He was drafted with the third overall pick in the 2007 NBA draft by the Atlanta Hawks, a team he played nine seasons with before signing with the Celtics as a free agent in the 2016 off-season. After playing three seasons with the Celtics, he signed with the 76ers in the 2019 off-season and played a season with the team before being traded in the 2020 off-season to the Thunder.

Throughout its long and fruitful history, the NBA has been all about the big man's game for a majority of its dominance in the world of basketball. From the 1950's, the very first Laker legend George Mikan ruled the paint with his 6'9" frame, though he would likely be an undersized centre in today's league. Then, there were legends of the 60's, Bill Russell and Wilt Chamberlain, who were both the centres of attention during their era of basketball, particularly with how they were causing tremors on the hard floor whenever they were banging bodies.

Russell was always a defensive juggernaut that could alter anybody's shot, body up just about any other big man, and collect rebounds like his life depended on it. On the other hand, Chamberlain was the very first unstoppable force in the league. Standing 7'1" and weighing about 300 pounds, he was too big, strong, and athletic for anyone to handle in his era of basketball. Bill and Wilt were two of the first players that made basketball a league dominated by big men, especially with how they were winning MVP's and championships in the process.

Fast forward to a decade later, Lew Alcindor, who would later be known as Kareem Abdul-Jabbar, towered over other centres and used his patented sky hook to score against the longest and strongest centres in the league. In a career that spanned two decades, Kareem would win six MVP's and numerous NBA titles while garnering the top spot for most points scored in a career. Still, in his era and up to the 80's, the big centre position was always thought of as the most important role in the NBA.

Following the footsteps of some of the early centres in the league were Moses Malone, Hakeem Olajuwon, David Robinson, and Shaquille O'Neal, who all won titles and MVP awards from the 80's to the 90's because of how well they crowded and dominated the paint. Even though the NBA has gone past its 50th year anniversary, no other position in the league has ever been more celebrated or influential than the centre spot.

However, since the dawn of the new millennium, the NBA has seen a shortage of dominant low post players as the league slowly but steadily transitioned into a game more suitable for guards and smaller forwards. And while the NBA, for the longest time, was all about scoring inside the paint using the biggest players in the team, games have become contests of whoever makes more outside shots or whoever had the more athletic perimeter players. And, in a matter of time, the era of the centre's dominance of basketball was all but over.

Today, teams would rather focus their attention towards developing their guards and forwards rather than their big men. Centres today are usually confined to the role of shot blocker or rebounder rather than the old concept of them being the first options on offense. Some teams would even hand the centre position over to smaller yet more mobile players for them to keep up with the quickening pace of the NBA today. The centre position has even disappeared in the All-Star voting system as it was replaced with the term "frontcourt players." As years went by, the conventional definition and role of the centre has all but changed or even disappeared.

Though the definition of what it means to be a centre in today's NBA has changed, there are still a few remnants of the past in some of today's big men. They are still able to play like the traditional centres of old, who could dominate the paint with their scoring, rebounding, and defence. They also adjust their style to fit the modern game of basketball regarding speed, pace, and outside shooting. One of those centres is Al Horford.

Since joining the NBA in 2007, Al Horford has always been a productive starter at the centre position from whatever spot on the floor he was at. Standing 6'10", he was never the biggest centre on the floor. He once played in an era when gigantic centres such as Shaquille O'Neal and Yao Ming roamed the paint. Back then, though he was always a centre, one may even qualify Horford's size and skillset as one belonging to a power forward instead.

However, in today's game, Horford's size has suited him fairly well considering that the league has had a shortage of dominant big men down low. And, at 245 pounds, Horford has the right combination of strength and mobility to make sure he could push anyone down on the low block while also keeping up with quicker big men.

As a former member of the Atlanta Hawks, Horford has long been one of the team's best players, if not their best and most consistent. In a team that has played a systematic brand basketball throughout the years, Al Horford's abilities to play the post, hit open jump shots, defend the paint, and make timely passes have been instrumental in the Hawks' consistent playoff appearances in the centre's tenure with the team. Now with the Celtics, Al Horford was one of the most sought after players at his position in free agency and is one of the highest-paid centres in the league due to his ability to fit with any system and adjust to today's style of basketball.

Born in the Dominican Republic, Al Horford is also one of the best international centres that plays in the NBA and other worldwide competitions all over the globe. He has always been a fixture for the Dominican Republic's national basketball team and has dominated in international tournaments across the world as his country's best player. Though the Dominican Republic is still a growing nation as far as of basketball is concerned, Al Horford has helped his country grow in that sport and is surely one of the players that would usher their team to new heights in future international competitions while he continues to rise in an evolving game of basketball.

CHAPTER 1: CHILDHOOD, EARLY LIFE, AND HIGH SCHOOL CAREER

Alfred "Al" Horford was born on June 3, 1986, in San Felipe de Puerto Plata, Puerto de Plata in the Dominican Republic. Al was born to parents Alfredo William "Tito" Horford and Arelis Reynoso. Tito Horford himself was once a basketball star, having played in the NBA for three seasons. At 7'1", he was a large centre and was the first player from the Dominican Republic to play in the NBA after getting selected 39th overall by the Milwaukee Bucks back in 1988 when Al was only two years old.

Tito, who started playing basketball at a young age in the Dominican Republic, was recruited by a Houston-based high school until he was good enough to get a spot on Louisiana State University's basketball team before getting cut without playing a single minute. He then spent the next two years with the University of Miami where he averaged 14.2 points and 9.3 rebounds over the course of the next two seasons. Tito then played limited minutes in his stint with the Bucks in the NBA. He played 60 games for them while barely playing over 6 minutes a night. Then, during the 1993-94 season, he was signed by the Washington Bullets after a few seasons of playing overseas. However, he would only play three games that year.

Al Horford's mother, Arelis Reynoso, is a journalist by profession, and she has always been a staunch supporter of her son's basketball dreams ever since the eldest Horford child was in his early years.

For the young Al Horford, life as a young boy was not so easy considering all the travels he had to make while Tito was playing professionally in the USA and other foreign basketball leagues around the world. When Al was five years old, the family was in Italy when Tito was playing in the Italian league. And when he was a few months over the age of six, the Horford family was living in Brazil when the patriarch of the family was playing on that side of the world.

When the family moved back to the Dominican Republic, Al's mother enrolled him in a baseball league for recreational activities during the young boy's free time. However, Al would plead with his mother to never take him to that league ever again because he wanted to focus on basketball. Growing up watching his dad play the sport, Al Horford fell instantly in love with basketball while also idolizing the usual greats such as Shaquille O'Neal and all the other All-Star centres of that era. As Reynoso would remember, Al told her how much he wanted to learn and focus on basketball because, someday, he would play in the NBA.[1]

At first, Reynoso was uncomfortable with the idea of letting her son focus all of his energy on basketball because, on her part, she wanted Al to play baseball professionally. However, she would still support her child's dreams and enrolled Al Horford in the Escuela de Baloncesto de Leandro de la Cruz, a known school for basketball in the Dominican Republic. Soon after, he would go to the Colegio De La Salle in his fourth grade until he was ready for high school.

Much like his father, Al wanted to go to the United States for high school to better learn the sport of basketball and train himself to be ready for a college career in the NCAA. Armed with the blessing of his mother, who always encouraged him to reach for his dreams, Al Horford would go to Michigan, where his father and brother were, to go to high school and work hard for his goal of making it to the NBA.

The Horford family would relocate to Lansing, Michigan, where Al would play out his high school years. By the time he enrolled in Grand Ledge High School, Al Horford's NBA pedigree was already apparent. He was already so skillful for his age that he immediately became Grand Ledge's poster boy. Horford became so dominant in high school that he held seven school records in his four years in Grand Ledge.

By the time when Al Horford was a senior, Horford holds seven school records, including most career points (1,239). He was named Class A Player of the Year after averaging 21 points, 13 rebounds and five blocks per game. While at Grand Ledge, Horford played AAU basketball for the Michigan Mustangs, who were runners-up in the Adidas Big Time National Tournament. Considered a four-star recruit by Rivals.com, Horford was listed as the No. 7 power forward and the No. 36 player in the nation in 2004. when he was coming into college.

CHAPTER 2: COLLEGE CAREER

Horford accepted an athletic scholarship to attend the University of Florida, where he played for coach Billy Donovan and teamed up alongside Joakim Noah, Corey Brewer and Taurean Green. At the helm of the Gators was head coach Billy Donovan, who had done a remarkable job with the team ever since he joined the squad in 1996. For his part, he was on his way to an even better career as coach of the Florida Gators considering that he had four future NBA players coming in as freshmen.

Led by Al Horford, the Gators were hoping to bank on the potentials of the likes of their freshmen, namely Joakim Noah, Corey Brewer, and Taurean Green. However, among those four players, it was Horford who stood out for the Gators because it took him no time to adjust to the college style of basketball and make it to Florida's starting squad.

Al Horford was still about 6'8" at that time, but he already had the strength to match up with opposing big men alongside senior and future NBA standout David Lee on the talented frontcourt of the Gators. He would start 25 of Florida's 32 games that season while averaging 5.6 points, 6.5 rebounds, and 1.6 blocks. Al Horford's defensive presence in the middle was key considering that he led the Gators in blocks that season on their way to a Southeastern Conference Championship heading to the NCAA tournament. However, the Gators would lose to a lower-seeded team in March Madness, though their future as a squad was bright. Their freshmen gained valuable experience throughout the season.

With David Lee moving on to become an NBA player the following season, it was Joakim Noah who replaced him at the starting position while Al Horford was relegated to the power forward spot to give the Florida Gators a fearsome defensive frontcourt. Meanwhile, Green and Brewer were out on the perimeter doing most of the scoring for the Gators while their big men defended the paint.

The Florida Gators, with the help of their fearsome frontcourt, dominated the SEC from the get-go by registering 17 consecutive victories to star the season. Those involved wins against even the toughest teams in the conference that the Gators made to look like high school teams. The Gators would again make the NCAA tournament after finishing the SEC tournament with another title.

Al Horford's presence on the defensive end was one of the keys to the Gators' dominant performance in their conference. He upped his scoring average to 11.3 points while shooting an impressive 60% from the floor. Al was also the Gators' leading rebounder with 7.6 boards a game while making his presence felt on the defensive end, averaging one steal and 1.7 blocks per outing. His passing skills were also apparent after averaging 2.0 assists per game that season. Horford, because of his performance, would be named to the All-SEC Second Team.

Al Horford and his Florida Gators would be even more dominant once the NCAA tournament started. As the third seed heading into March Madness, the Gators would go out and win the first two rounds with relative ease. Then, after a tough win against Georgetown in the Sweet Sixteen, the Gators would get easy wins against Villanova and George Mason heading into the NCAA Finals.

The Florida Gators would meet the UCLA Bruins in the National Championship Game with all the stakes on the line. It was then and there when Al Horford emerged as a star for the Gators. He dominated the paint with his 14 points and 7 rebounds to edge out UCLA and win the NCAA Tournament title and a Final Four All-Tournament selection as a consolation to the performance that he put up in the final games of March Madness.

The following season, Al Horford and the Florida Gators sported the same starting lineup and were just as hungry as they were when they won the title a year before. The Gators would win six straight to start the season, but would lose the surging Horford for a few games in December because of injury. This led Billy Donovan to rest his star big man for more games until December 23 in time for a matchup with a much improved Ohio State squad led by dominant 7-foot freshman Greg Oden.

A day before the hyped matchup between Florida and Ohio, Donovan would announce that Horford would be unable to play in the game because of the injury he had been resting. But, during the match, when Greg Oden was muscling his way through every defender put on him, Donovan suddenly inserted the Dominican Republic's finest young player to put on a defensive show against the gigantic Ohio centre. Despite nearly three inches of height and 50 pounds of weight between the two big men, Horford stood up against the highly-touted freshman to limit Oden's production. The potential top pick in the 2007 NBA Draft would only score 7 points because of Horford's defence. Meanwhile, Al, who came off the bench, had 11 points and 11 rebounds in that game.

With another SEC Tournament title under their belts, the top-ranked Florida Gators were just as unbeatable in the NCAA tournament as they were a season ago. Their status was mostly thanks to the increased production of their best player, Al Horford, who averaged 13.2 points, 9.5 rebounds, 2.2 assists, and 1.8 blocks the entire regular season for the Gators. He was even better in the SEC tournament, norming 14 points and 11 boards in those games.

The Florida Gators would make the NCAA Championship Game again after their stellar showing in the Tournament. Against the UCLA Bruins in the Final Four, Horford would only attempt three shots all game along as he focused on the defensive end of the floor to beat the previous season's co-finalists by 10 points. He had 9 points and 17 rebounds in that team effort.

Matched up against Ohio State's Greg Oden in the Championship Game, Al Horford was in a battle between the two best big men in the collegiate ranks. While Oden was better when the two big men first met, Al Horford came into the title game with a cast of more talented players than what the potential top overall pick had.

Despite sporting a group of well-rounded players, Horford came out as the best of the bunch in Florida's fearsome foursome. He ended the game with 18 points, 12 rebounds, three assists, and two blocks to lead the Gators past Ohio State and Oden, who had 25 points and 12 rebounds, to become the first team since the Duke Blue Devils in the early 90's to win back-to-back National Championships. And shortly after winning the title, the four juniors led by Horford all declared for the 2007 NBA Draft.

CHAPTER 3: NBA CAREER

Getting Drafted

After three successful years resulting in two national titles with Florida State, Al Horford was already more than ready to ply his wares in the NBA, where his father sparingly played during Tito Horford's younger years. However, Al, though not as tall as his father, was far better a player than the first Dominican Republic player to make it to the NBA. Al's quality and pedigree as a future star in the big leagues were already apparent in his three years of college basketball.

Listed at about 6'10" and weighing slightly under 250 pounds, Al Horford was NBA ready as far as size was concerned for a young man that played power forward for the majority of his basketball career. And at that size, Horford was big enough to play centre, which he did during a few stretches in college, especially when he was guarding the likes of Greg Oden at the low post or when he was defending the basket from inside incursions. Horford also showed excellent strength during the pre-draft combine when he outmuscled every other player that bench pressed.

Size and strength were not the only things going for Al Horford. Despite his size, Al could run the floor pretty well and was able to beat most of his matchups to his position during offensive sets. And with his 35-inch vertical, Horford is one of the more athletic big men in the 2007 NBA Draft class, especially considering that it did not look like he could run quickly or jump high off the court because of his size.[2]

Offensively, Al Horford's athleticism and mobility for a big man were what set him apart from all the other power forwards and centres in the draft class. He could run the floor and finish in transition or beat his man to the basket. Other than that, Al was seen to have a good touch inside the paint, especially when he shot above 60% in his final two seasons with the Gators. Most of that good touch around the basket was a product of his upper body strength when finishing under the rim. And when the lane got clogged, Horford had shown the ability to hit close perimeter jumpers when needed.

Probably the best thing about Al Horford's offensive capabilities was the fact that he was always willing to listen to his coach and always ready to improve. Horford's offensive production and skill level around the basket was always improving since the day he joined the Florida Gators. His basketball IQ allows him to learn from his coaches quickly and use new skills to make his mark on the basketball court. Moreover, regarding his demeanour, Al was always calm on the court. He never tried to do more than what he was capable of, nor did his emotions ever get the best of him. Horford always knew where he was, what he needed to do, and who he needed to go to, no matter what the situation was.

While putting baskets through the hoop is what it takes to win games, defence is what is always what is needed to win championships. Al Horford was never short of defence, and that was why he won two national titles in Florida. The big Dominican player excels at clogging the paint with his broad shoulders and making life difficult for opposing big men by using his size and strength to defend them down at the low post. He was able to hold his own against the bigger Greg Oden in their first meeting, though he struggled to contain him during the championship game. Nevertheless, Horford's anticipation skills and leaping ability were also what made him an excellent defender, even back in the collegiate ranks. He knows when to rotate to the weak side to block or intimidate shots to the full length of his wingspan and jumping ability.

Defence is never done until you get the rebound. Al Horford also showed an excellent nose for the ball when going up for rebounds. He has led the Florida Gators in rebounding since his sophomore year even as he was playing with the taller and equally skilled rebounder in Joakim Noah at the frontcourt. Al never backed down whenever he would pursue rebounds, and his upper body strength and large frame helped him get the job done. He was even seen going toe to toe with Greg Oden in the rebounding department back in the championship game as the two heavily favoured draftees both collected boards in bunches.

Despite three years of playing at a high level in college, Al Horford was still as raw as one could get coming into the NBA. Though he was able to shoot above 60% from the floor in his final two seasons in Florida, Horford was all about strength and finishing ability in getting his inside scoring opportunities. He was still very raw as far as post moves were concerned and was yet to develop a go-to move down at the low block. He does not have the footwork of a dominant post player like a Tim Duncan or a Hakeem Olajuwon, and still needed work in that department.

That was why, in the championship game, Al Horford was often seen trying to score most of his points from the perimeter instead of the paint considering that he could not use his size against the bigger Oden. It was only when the Ohio big man was out of the game when Horford was seen attacking the basket. Speaking of the perimeter, Horford's midrange shooting still needed work, though the potential for him to hit those jumpers was already there.

Though Al Horford has shown a good basketball IQ, his mentality was somewhat questionable. Among the four Florida Gators that made it to the NBA, Horford was the most talented out of the bunch, but he was not as confident as the other three on the offensive end. He was bigger, stronger, and more refined than Joakim Noah, but he would rather defer to his frontcourt mate at times. And instead of establishing himself as an unstoppable force inside the paint, he would defer to his perimeter teammates in certain stretches.

Another questionable aspect of his mental approach to the game was his consistency. There were games when Al Horford was simply a beast on the floor, but then he would drift in the next two games, showing subpar numbers in the process. At his best, Al was one of the best big men in the country. But for the rest of the games, he was as mediocre as any other third string big man out there.

Lastly, Al Horford was a tweener back in college. He was listed as a power forward, but would sometimes play centre. He had the size of a centre and the skills of a power forward, but he might be outmatched by the bigger centres or by the quicker and more skilled power forwards in the NBA. And that was why, based on his skillset and preferred playing position, Horford was often compared to tweener power forwards like Horace Grant and Carlos Boozer, though those players did not have the defensive capabilities that the Dominican Republic native had.

As good a prospect as Al Horford was coming into the NBA, the only question was how far below the first two spots would he fall. The central question of the 2007 NBA Draft was who between dominant big man Greg Oden and standout transcendent scorer Kevin Durant was more deserving to be the top overall pick. There was no question that those two players would end up with the first two picks of that year's draft. However, every pick below the second one was a mystery as the talent difference between all the other projected lottery pick was slim. Those players included Al Horford's Florida teammates Corey Brewer and Joakim Noah. It was rather a question of what kind of a player the team needed rather than the players' talent that would determine who would go third and below in the draft.

To no one's surprise, Greg Oden and Kevin Durant were picked number one and two respectively. With the Atlanta Hawks up on the clock with the third pick of the draft, most analysts had them pegged to pick either Al Horford or Mike Conley from Ohio State. One might consider that the Hawks did not need another big man since Zaza Pachulia and Josh Smith were already crowding the paint. At best, they needed a point guard like Mike Conley considering that they deeply lacked in that position as far as production was concerned. However, despite their need for a talented playmaker, the Hawks decided to draft Al Horford with the third pick, figuring they needed more youth and size on the frontcourt. And with that, Al continued the Horford family tradition and fulfilled his dreams of making it to the NBA.

Rookie Season

On June 28, 2007, Horford was selected by the Atlanta Hawks with the third overall pick in the 2007 NBA draft. On July 9, he signed his rookie scale contract with the Hawks. The Atlanta Hawks were not in the best shape to win a title or even contend for a playoff spot when Al Horford joined the team. Considering they were bad enough in the previous season to get the third pick in the 2007 NBA Draft, they were not expected to suddenly become contenders just by adding a few pieces and a raw but promising rookie like Al Horford.

But with head coach Mike Woodson trusting the young Al Horford enough, he immediately inserted the two-time national champion to the starting squad as the team's centre, though he was accustomed to playing the power forward spot during his earlier years as a player. Thrusting Horford to the starting centre position gave the Hawks an athletic but undersized frontline composed of the Florida Gators standout and the 22-year-old Josh Smith.

As a starter, Al Horford immediately paid dividends for the Hawks, who loved the defence and rebounding tenacity that the Dominican Republic native provided them. Al started his NBA career with a win over the Dallas Mavericks on November 2, 2007. In just a little under 23 minutes of action, he had 9 points and ten rebounds. After that, he battled against the physical frontline of the Detroit Pistons to grab a total of 11 rebounds while nearly beating one of the favourites in the Eastern Conference that season.

Early on, Al Horford immediately showed his strengths on the rebounding and defensive ends of the court, though his offense was still a work in progress. In just his third game, he had four steals and two blocks in a narrow loss to the New Jersey Nets before collecting a then-season and career high of 15 rebounds to go along with 8 points and two blocks in the Hawks' win over the Phoenix Suns on November 7. Then, in a loss to the Celtics in the next game, he had his first double-digit scoring performance of 16 points on 5 out of 12 shooting.

Over the course of the next three games, Al Horford wowed crowds with his ability to control the boards with double-digit rebounding in those outings. In a win against the Charlotte Bobcats, Al had his first double-double game of the season when he put up 13 points and 13 rebounds while also outplaying former top overall pick and 2005 Rookie of the Year centre Emeka Okafor over at the other end.

Then, in a clash between the second and third picks of the 2007 NBA Draft, the Seattle SuperSonics and Atlanta Hawks battled each other to two overtime periods. Though Kevin Durant won the clash, Horford still finished with a remarkable line of 7 points, 14 rebounds, and five blocks in 53 minutes of action. Then, in his first clash with the gigantic legend Shaquille O'Neal, one of his idols growing up, Horford would not even start as the bigger Pachulia was more fit to guard Shaq. Al would still guard him for most of the game, though he would struggle. Horford only had 6 points and eight rebounds while O'Neal had 18 points, ten rebounds, and seven blocks. Al was still good enough for the whole month of November to be named the Eastern Rookie of the Month.

On December 3, Al Horford would put up his second double-double performance of the season when he finished a win against the Philadelphia 76ers with 12 points and 13 rebounds. He shot 6 out of 9 from the field in that game. That was after he tied a season high of 15 rebounds the previous match. He would then finish the next three games with double-digit rebounding to mount a streak of five double-digit rebound games.

In a win over the Utah Jazz on December 17, Al Horford recorded a new season and career high in points when he scored 17 on 8 out of 11 shooting. He also added seven rebounds in that game. While failing to show up concerning stats for the majority of the month of December, Al made good of himself in January. He was instrumental in beating the Cleveland Cavaliers on January 9, 2008, with his 10 points and 15 rebounds. After that game, he collected 19 boards in a loss to the Washington Wizards to increase his career-high in that department.

Horford would finish January with five double-digit rebounding performances in five of his final six games that month. He had two double-doubles in those six outings. The first was when he had 14 points, 11 rebounds, and five steals in a loss to the Denver Nuggets on January 23. Two days later, he delivered 10 points and 16 rebounds in a win against the Seattle Sonics.

Al Horford was even better in February. He started that month by scoring 14 in a win over the Nets while being an instrumental part of two more wins after that game. In their third consecutive win, which was against the Los Angeles Lakers, Horford had a career night. Matched up against the taller and more experienced Pau Gasol, Al finished the win with 15 points and a new career high of 20 rebounds to solidify his name as one of the top rookies that season.

However, Horford would still show that he was still a rookie in need of refining when he struggled against the much bigger Yao Ming on February 9. Yao scored over the much shorter man and finished with 28 points. Meanwhile, Al only had 8 points and eight rebounds. And although they were losses, Horford had back-to-back double-doubles against the Pistons and the Bobcats on February 12 and 13 respectively. He averaged 12 points and 15 rebounds in those two games.

Al Horford made his way to the All-Star Weekend as part of the Rookie Team that challenged the Sophomore stars of the NBA. The Rookies would lose, but Horford was second in scoring for his team. He finished with 19 points and seven rebounds. Al then rounded up February with a new career best of 20 points together with 11 rebounds in a win over the New York Knicks on the 29th day of the month. Rightfully enough, he was named Rookie of the Month for the second occasion that season.

Starting to finally find his groove with the Hawks after adjusting to the more physical style of the NBA game, Horford began to show flashes of his future All-Star self with consistent double-double performances for the month of March. On March 7, he had 18 points and 11 rebounds in a loss to the Bobcats. Ten days later, he was all over the place in a win against the Wizards when he finished the game with 12 points, 15 rebounds, six assists, and two blocks. He was even better in a loss to the Nets in the next game when he had 20 points, 15 rebounds, and six assists. And in the final two games of March, he averaged 18.5 points and 9.5 rebounds to contribute to the Hawks' winning streak and to get named the Rookie of the Month again.

Al Horford would round up his regular season as a rookie with four double-digit rebounding games in his final four games. Two of those were double-double performances that saw him scoring 19 and 17 points respectively against the Knicks and the Celtics. Needless to say, Al Horford was quickly becoming an integral part of the Atlanta Hawks' future.

In his rookie season, Al Horford nearly averaged a double-double when he normed 10.1 points and 9.7 rebounds. The Dominican Republic native would shoot about 50% from the field to showcase his efficiency inside the paint. He led the Hawks in rebounding all season long while finishing second to Kevin Durant in voting for the Rookie of the Year award. Despite the close runner-up finish in that regard, Horford was the best rookie big man of the 2007 Draft class after being the only unanimous member of the All-Rookie First Team. With Greg Oden out that season because of injury, Horford established himself as the finest centre of his draft class and as a perennial winner after being an instrumental part of the Hawks' return to the playoffs as the eighth seed in the East.

In Game 1 against the top-seeded and historically great 2007-08 Boston Celtics squad composed of Hall of Fame players like Kevin Garnett, Paul Pierce, and Ray Allen, Al Horford was the lone bright spot against such a powerhouse team. He would finish the game with 20 points and ten rebounds while holding his own against a big veteran frontline of Garnett and Kendrick Perkins. However, the Hawks would lose that game by 23. But it was not a bad outing for a rookie playing his first playoff game.

Game 2 was not all that different as far as results were concerned for the Atlanta Hawks. The Celtics were too talented and experienced for the younger squad. The Celtic frontline was also able to limit Horford to 9 points and nine rebounds after the Atlanta centre was able to do well in his playoff debut. Down 0-2, the Hawks seemed like a team out of the running early.

Things started to get gritty when the series moved over to Atlanta. The core of the Hawks began to move the ball fluidly as their unselfish style of basketball found open men for easy shots. Horford himself was an integral part of that fluid game. The rookie centre would finish the game with 17 points, 14 rebounds, and six assists in a victory where all of the Hawks' starters were in double digits. Save for Marvin Williams, every starter for Atlanta had at least six assists.

With his first playoff victory, Al Horford was looking to add more to his experience in the postseason. Focusing his energy on defence and rebounding in Game 4 despite his struggles from the floor, Al was able to add up to his team's wins against the Celtics after he finished with 13 rebounds. Against such a talented team, no one expected the gritty Hawks to tie the series two wins apiece.

The two wins at home propelled Al Horford to another good game in the series after he finished Game 5 with 14 points, ten rebounds, and five assists. But Boston was able to find their offense against the gritty defence played by Atlanta to regain composure and the hold on the series. But again, the Hawks fought back. Horford was one of six Atlanta players to score in double digits after he ended Game 6 with 16 points to go along with five rebounds, four assists, and three blocks. No one thought they were stingy enough to force Game 7.

The Boston Celtics, ever the experienced veteran All-Star team, dug deep into their hunger for a title to finally put away the pesky Atlanta Hawks in seven games. The Celtic defence kept the Hawks at bay after only two of their players scored in double digits. Al Horford was not one of them. Nevertheless, the rookie centre made good of himself in those seven games after averaging a double-double against the eventual NBA champions. Al normed 12.6 points, 10.4 rebounds, and 3.6 assists in his first playoff series.

Rising With Atlanta

In his rookie season, Al Horford did not average monstrous numbers, nor did he even take the league the storm with highlight reel plays. He simply played within the system while focusing on his role of rebounding, defending, and timely scoring. His consistency on both ends of the floor as far as his role was concerned was one of the keys to the Hawks' stellar showing against the Boston Celtics in the first round of the playoffs. With the Atlanta Hawks running on the high of their confident performance against the 2008 champions, the sky was going to be the limit for them in the upcoming seasons. And for Horford, he was just getting better with experience.

Right on cue, the Hawks did indeed play a lot better in the new season than they did the previous one. They would open the 2008-09 season with six consecutive wins. The man in the middle, Al Horford, was primarily responsible for some of those wins. While never the dominant post scorer, Horford played his role to perfection in the first few games of the season as he rebounded the ball with regularity while dishing out four assists per game in the Hawks' first three wins.

In the fifth game of the season, Horford was a vital piece of the defence that helped the Hawks beat the rising Oklahoma City Thunder, formerly the Seattle Sonics. He finished that win with 12 rebounds and five blocks. Then, against the Chicago Bulls in the next game, he would have a career night to help his team win their sixth straight of the season. Al Horford finished with 27 points, 17 rebounds, and six blocks to show what he was capable of when he was at his best.

Though the Atlanta Hawks could not sustain the amount of wins they had in the opening segments of the season, they would remain a competitive team throughout the season. Horford himself could not put up the same monstrous numbers that he had in Chicago but did his best to maintain his stand as one of the brightest young centres in the league. On November 26 in a win against the Milwaukee Bucks, he had 21 points, nine rebounds, two assists, two steals, and three blocks for a well-rounded stat line for a centre. Three days later when the Hawks won over the Wizards, Al finished the game with 19 points, 13 rebounds, six assists, two steals, and one block. He then ended seven straight games of scoring in double digits with his 14 points in a loss to the Houston Rockets on December 9.

While Al Horford was obviously better and more experienced compared to when he was a rookie, consistency on a regular basis was still something he had to work on as his numbers mirrored that of his rookie stats. However, he was the main contributor to the Hawks' six-game run to end the year 2008. He had four double-doubles in those six wins, had at least one block in each of those wins, and was a factor in distributing the ball. His best performance out of the bunch was when he finished a blowout in Denver with 16 points, ten rebounds, and four assists.

Consistency was still something that Al Horford was still lacking on a regular basis, and considering that he missed the majority of January 2009 because of injury, it would take a while for him to get back to the near All-Star level he was once playing at. He returned on February 4 after nearly four weeks of absence. His numbers in the Rising Stars Challenge during All-Star Weekend were not even as good as the ones he put up in his rookie season. However, Al would find his groove shortly after the midseason break when he posted 18 points, 18 rebounds, four assists, and two blocks in a win over the Sacramento Kings on February 18.

Then, on February 25, Al Horford was as good as advertised and showed he was back to full health when he had 21 points, 11 rebounds, and three steals in a narrow loss to the Nuggets. But it was the game following that one when Horford truly showed flashes of his peak form. In a win against the Miami Heat on February 27, the Dominican Republic native finished the game with 21 points and 22 massive rebounds for his first 20-20 game.

After that career game against Miami, Horford would not slow down as he would score in double digits in 11 of the Hawks' next 13 games. He had nine double-doubles at that juncture as the Atlanta Hawks would only lose four of those games. Al's best performance in that stretch for the Hawks was when he had 23 points, 12 rebounds, and six assists against the Sacramento Kings in a blowout win on March 17. He shot 9 out of 13 from the floor and played only 33 minutes that game.

Over the course of the Atlanta Hawks' final ten games, Al Horford had five double-digit rebounding games as well as five games of scoring at least 13 points. In the Hawks' second to the last game of the season, Horford unleashed 22 points, 15 rebounds, five assists, two steals, and one block in a win over the Pacers to cap off stellar outings for him after the All-Star break.

Horford's numbers at the end of the season did not reflect how good he was, especially right after the All-Star Weekend. His stats would mirror that of his rookie season as he averaged 11.5 points, 9.3 rebounds, 2.4 assists, and 1.4 blocks in his second year in the NBA. However, he would shoot a lot better from the floor after norming a clip of 52.5%. Horford's presence in the middle on both ends of the floor was also a reason for Atlanta's improved 47-35 record. They would make the playoffs with the fourth seed in the East after qualifying as the eighth seed the previous season.

In Game 1 of the Atlanta Hawks' first-round matchup against the Miami Heat, Al Horford was integral in keeping the opposing big men at bay while making sure he was outplaying veterans Jermaine O'Neal and Udonis Haslem. He would end the game as the third-leading scorer for the Hawks after putting up 14 points together with nine rebounds and two blocks.

Unfortunately for Al Horford, the Miami Heat's big men found a way to score inside baskets over the less experienced Hawks centre. Both O'Neal and Haslem were getting easy shots inside the paint to the detriment of Horford, so much so that the second year centre became a liability despite his double-double effort. After that Game 2 loss, the Hawks' interior was again thoroughly demolished by the Heat's veteran frontcourt duo. Both O'Neal and Haslem ended that blowout Heat win with double-double performances while Horford could neither contain their inside scoring nor their rebounding efforts.

Realizing that their interior was their biggest liability against the Miami Heat in Games 2 and 3, the Atlanta Hawks mixed things up and decided to play Al Horford limited minutes in favour of the bigger and more experienced Zaza Pachulia. Pachulia would end the game with 12 points and 18 rebounds while doing a much better job at containing the Heat's big men compared to what Horford did in the last two games. Al would only play less than 17 minutes in Game 4 while tallying 4 points and three rebounds in that Atlanta win.

The Hawks used the same approach to win Game 5 and to regain the series lead. Al Horford had 3 points and four rebounds in less than 12 minutes in that game. This time, it was not because Al was a liability. It was because he had to leave the game with an injured right ankle after he was fouled hard and landed on his right leg in an awkward fashion early in the first half.

Needless to say, Al Horford's presence in Game 6 was badly missed as the Miami Heat's Dwyane Wade continuously sliced through the lane to get baskets in the paint and to finish the game with 41 points and a win. None of the Hawks' backup centres could produce the same kind of all-around efforts that Al could provide on a nightly basis. But despite the pain in the ankle, Horford made a return in Game 7 when his team badly needed him. He was obviously still feeling the effects of the injury after a subpar performance from him. Luckily, the Hawks went to their All-Star leader Joe Johnson to lead them past the Miami Heat and on to the second round for the first time since 1999.

Coming into the series against the heavily favoured Cleveland Cavaliers, Al Horford was still seriously bothered by the ankle sprain he suffered in the first round against the Miami Heat. His mobility was hampered while the Cavs' much bigger frontline pounded him on the boards. Horford would finish with 4 points and eight rebounds in 25 minutes in that blowout loss.

Al Horford would miss Game 2 because of the effects of the sprained ankle he injured back in the first round, and as expected, the Cavaliers steamrolled past them in that game. Al would make a return to play in Games 3 and 4 only in futile outings for him and the Hawks. The injury and the superior defensive capabilities of the Cavs limited Horford to a total of 6 points and 7 rebounds in Game 3 and 4, which Cleveland won in easy fashion.

While the outcome might have been the same, the Hawks might not have gotten swept out of the second round had their starting centre been at his best health. Horford would average poor numbers of 6.9 points and 5.8 rebounds in the 2009 postseason. The bright side was that Al had become an important part of the Atlanta Hawks, who surprisingly improved by leaps and bounds as their starting centre got better and more experienced.

First All-Star Season

No longer hobbled by the ankle sprain that hampered him for the majority of the 2009 playoffs, Al Horford came into the 2009-10 season as one of the best, if not the most important players in the Atlanta Hawks' line-up. That line-up featured the addition of reliable sixth man Jamal Crawford and future All-Star point guard Jeff Teague.

Horford would start the new season by dominating the much bigger Roy Hibbert of the Indiana Pacers on both ends of the court. He used his superior skillset and mobility to score baskets against the gigantic centre to finish with 24 points, 16 rebounds, four assists, and two blocks for the winning Hawks. After that, he dominated the Wizards on the defensive end by providing five blocks alongside his 10 points and 12 rebounds.

On November 11 against former Florida Gators teammate David Lee of the New York Knicks, Horford put up a new season high of 25 points on 9 out of 16 shooting while also contributing nine rebounds, three assists, two steals, and two blocks in that win. Al was not the only one having a good start to the season as his Atlanta Hawks won 11 of their first 13 games. In those 13 games, Horford had seven double-double performances that all came in wins. He scored in double digits in all but that loss against LA Lakers in their third game of the season as he struggled against the bigger frontline of the purple and gold.

As a model of efficiency for the Hawks, Al Horford was able to provide good numbers despite the limited touches he saw on the offensive end while relying mostly on good ball movement and timely inside incursions for his scoring opportunities. No one was more efficient than he was on December 2 in a blowout win against the Toronto Raptors after he finished the game with 24 points on 10 out of 12 shooting in only 23 minutes of action. And though the next game was a loss, he did dominate the Knicks frontline anew with his 17 points and 14 rebounds.

As December went along, it was becoming ever more apparent that Al Horford was an All-Star on the rise. He was grabbing attention then and there with his efficient play on both ends of the floor while sustaining his hold as one of the brightest young centres in the league. Together with the consistently rising Hawks, Al was able to help his team win six straight games in the middle of the month. All of those wins came in dominating fashion for Atlanta.

Horford also mounted four consecutive All-Star worthy double-double performances in the middle of December. It started when he had 15 points and 12 rebounds in a tightly contested overtime loss to the Chicago Bulls on December 19 and ended with the 25 points, 19 rebounds, and five blocks he put up against the Indiana Pacers on December 26 after he thoroughly decimated their bigger but slower frontline again. Though Horford was never the tallest centre on the floor, he had the mobility and skillset to outplay the slower giants.

The New Year started well for Al Horford on a personal level when he once again outclassed David Lee of the New York Knicks on the frontcourt. Taking advantage of his superior size, he drained 11 of his 14 shots from the field to score 22 points along with the 19 rebounds, four assists, and three blocks he collected. He meanwhile limited his matchup to 11 points and seven rebounds though the Knicks came out on top in overtime.

On January 15, Al Horford was matched up with the equally mobile but agiler centre Amar'e Stoudemire, who was just as big and powerful as he was. Though he was not able to match Stoudemire's production point for point and rebound for rebound, Horford came out with the win after putting up 24 points on 10 out of 13 shooting and grabbing nine rebounds in the process. Then, a week later, had 23 points, nine rebounds, and five assists against the Charlotte Bobcats in a win for the Hawks, who were beginning to fly higher than they ever had in the past few seasons.

Al was consistently putting up good numbers on both ends of the floor for the Atlanta Hawks and was making his team better with his inside presence. Because of that, Al Horford was selected as a reserve player in the 2010 Eastern All-Star squad to become the first ever player to be drafted by the Hawks since 1992 to make it to the midseason classic. In the All-Star Game, Horford would make 4 of his five attempts to score 8 points in his first appearance in the game reserved for the brightest of stars in the NBA.

The glitz and glamor of making his first All-Star appearance did not stop Al Horford from putting on great outings for his team. In the Hawks' first game back since the break, Horford matched up with fellow first-time All-Star Chris Kaman of the LA Clippers. Al proved to be the brighter star among the two when he finished the 18-point win with a new high of 31 points on 12 out of 15 shooting from the floor. He then went to the Bay Area to put up 26 points and 11 rebounds against the Golden State Warriors in a tight loss. After that, Horford was a model of consistency and would score in double digits in all of his games until April 9.

While pushing hard for a good playoff spot, Al Horford was becoming the Hawks' brightest star despite the fact that Joe Johnson was the established alpha male of the team. Nevertheless, Horford's potential was becoming even more apparent when he had 27 points and 15 rebounds on March 5 in a win against the Warriors. Eleven days later, he led a 29-point win against the New Jersey Nets with his 15 points, 11 rebounds, and seven assists. Al would proceed with the next seven games with consecutive double-double performances to cap a personal best of eight straight double-doubles.

One of Al Horford's better performances in that double-double streak was on March 21 when he was matched up against a childhood idol Tim Duncan. The Big Fundamental was able to outscore him in that match, but Al was phenomenal in the other aspects of the game after registering 22 points, 18 rebounds, and two steals in that win for the Atlanta Hawks. His double-double streak would come to its conclusion on March 28 after he dominated the Pacer frontline again with his 18 points and 12 rebounds. However, he would end his season strong by registering double-digit rebounding in all of the Hawks' final six games of the season.

At the end of his first All-Star season, Al Horford was norming numbers worthy of an All-Star centre in an NBA generation that was lacking dominant big men in the middle of the paint. He averaged 14.2 points, 9.9 rebounds, and 2.3 assists while shooting an efficient 55.1%, which ranked eighth overall in the NBA. He also finished 10th in rebounds after leading the Hawks with his 39 double-doubles, which ranked 11th overall at the end of the season. What was even better about his rise to All-Stardom was the fact that he brought his team with him. Atlanta finished with a 53-29 record that gave them the third seed in the Eastern Conference playoff picture.

Al Horford's defensive presence in the paint lorded over the undersized frontline of the Milwaukee Bucks in Game 1 of their matchup. Al had 15 points, seven rebounds, and five blocks in that win. Then, in Game 2, he did a lot of the scoring load on top of his defensive duties. He finished that win with 20 points, ten rebounds, two steals, and three blocks.

But, in Games 3 and 4 in Milwaukee, the Bucks relied on the 37-year old 6'9" veteran Kurt Thomas to try and limit the production of the then 23-year-old Al Horford. He was saddled to 10 points and three rebounds. Meanwhile, the Bucks managed to get a lot of help from their bench in that game to make the series a little more interesting. Game 4 was just as mediocre for Horford while the Bucks made it a series by winning two games at home.

Back in Atlanta, Horford tried to put the team on his back to deliver one of his best playoff performances to that date. He finished with 25 points, 11 rebounds, and two blocks though the Milwaukee Bucks won their third straight game to threaten the Hawks to a monumental first round meltdown. But the Atlanta Hawks found their composure in Games 6 and 7 while Horford manned and controlled the paint. The Hawks won both games by double digits with Al averaging 15.5 points, 15 rebounds, three assists, and two blocks in those two wins to reach the Conference Semi-Finals again for the second consecutive year.

The real test for Al Horford came in the second round of the 2010 playoffs when his team matched up against the Orlando Magic led by Dwight Howard, who was widely regarded as the best centre in the league during those years. Horford may have been a mobile and strong centre that was hard to match up with especially because of his defensive capabilities and broad skill set. However, Howard was much more athletic and might have been stronger and more dominant inside the paint than Al was.

The difference between the two young centres was evident in Game 1 when the Magic pounded the Hawks to a 43-point beat down. Horford was limited to 4 points and six rebounds while failing to contend with the 21 points, 12 rebounds, and five blocks of his matchup. But Al bounced back in Game 2 to show his class against a defensive expert like Dwight Howard. He had 24 points and ten rebounds to lead his team in scoring but failed once again to equal Howard, who had 29 points, 17 rebounds, and another win.

In Game 3, the problems of trying to contain Dwight Howard down at the post continued for the young and still improving Al Horford. Needless to say, he did not provide any impact for his team in another blowout loss while his matchup ran lose once again to show how wide the gap between the two best Eastern Conference centres was. The Magic would then finally put away the Hawks in a four-game sweep after another dominant performance in Game 4. Still, the young Hawks could not get a win in the second round even as their prized asset in the middle was healthier than he was the previous season. Horford, who had a better run in the playoffs that season, averaged 14.6 points and nine rebounds through 11 games.

Another All-Star Season, Another Second Round Exit

Because of the two consecutive sweeps to Eastern powerhouses, changes had to be made to the Atlanta Hawks. Management would fire Mike Woodson and replace him with long-time assistant coach Larry Drew to bring some changes to the Hawks that seemed to have already peaked under their former head coach. But the biggest move that management made in that offseason was signing Al Horford to a five-year extension worth $60 million, which was a discount considering how promising of a young centre the Dominican Republic native was.

Al Horford was featured more as a centrepiece of the offense under Larry Drew's system. He was running the offense through him and would often even make Horford run the offense from the post. This led to a great start, not only for the centre, but for the Hawks, who won six straight to open the season. Al was fantastic in that great start for Atlanta.

Though Horford would not make any significant noise in his first game, which was a blowout win against the Memphis Grizzlies, he started where he left off in the previous regular season by posting 20 points, 12 rebounds, three assists, and two blocks in his second game of the season. A day after that, on October 30, he had 21 points, ten rebounds, and three assists versus the Wizards. In the Hawks' 6-0 start, Horford had four excellent double-double performances.

On November 7 against the Phoenix Suns, Al Horford took no time to score at least 30 points for the first time that season. He had 30 points, ten rebounds, five assists, and two blocks in that game that saw him shooting 13 out of 16 from the field. However, that was the start of the Hawks' early season skid as they battled inconsistency and unfamiliarity with the new system.

After losing four straight games early, the Hawks would break the drought thanks to the efforts of their rising centre. On November 14, Al Horford would have 28 points, ten rebounds, and three blocks in a win over the Minnesota Timberwolves. Six days later in a loss to the Dallas Mavericks, Al finished the game with his first 20-20 outing of the season after posting 20 points and 20 rebounds to go along with five assists and three blocks.

Late in November up to early December, Horford was once again the centrepiece of another one of the Hawks' winning streaks. In that five-game run, he never scored under 15 points while collecting rebounds at a steady pace. But it was his playmaking that was even more impressive as Al Horford showed his class as a top distributor at the centre position. He had back-to-back games of dishing out six assists against Memphis and Philadelphia early in December. Then, shortly after the five-game run ended, he then had six assists again on top of the 24 points and ten rebounds he collected in a win against the New Jersey Nets on December 7.

After impressive all-around performances for the inconsistent Atlanta Hawks, Al Horford would reach a new high in assists when he dished out 8 of them in a win versus the Indiana Pacers on December 11. Horford also had 16 points and 16 rebounds in that game.

Then, later in the month, the Hawks would exact revenge on the two teams that tormented them the past two postseasons. They would win against the Orlando Magic and the Cleveland Cavaliers of course with their centre running things smoothly on both offense and defence. Horford would have 24 points, 11 rebounds, and four assists against the Magic before putting up 18 points, eight rebounds, and four dimes on the Cavs.

Come the New Year, Horford and his Hawks started another good run that had to end when their centre had his best all-around performance to date. Riding on a five-game run on January 15 against the Houston Rockets, scored and passed over the 6'6" centre Chuck Hayes for his 24 points, ten rebounds, and eight assists in a near triple-double effort. However, the run had to end there after Houston won by six. But in the very next game, Horford had another one of his great all-around performances. In a win against the Sacramento Kings, he finished with 23 points, nine rebounds, six assists, and a high of 7 blocks while matching up with another rising young centre in DeMarcus Cousins.

Then, against New York on January 28 shortly after missing a few games due to a minor injury, Al Horford had 19 points, 14 rebounds, and six assists. In the previous match, which was a loss to the Bucks, he had 17 points, ten rebounds, and five assists. At that moment, there probably was not a centre making assists more than Horford was. He even dished out seven dimes on February 2 in a win versus the Raptors on top of the 12 points and 14 rebounds he had.

Consistent performances on both ends of the floor and the way he was fast becoming the most important part of the Atlanta Hawks was how Al Horford was selected to his second consecutive All-Star Game appearance. As the only other centre in the line-up, there was no arguing that he was already the second best centre in the whole Eastern Conference. Only Dwight Howard was arguably better than him at that point. However, Horford would only contribute 2 points for the Eastern All-Stars in the midseason classic.

Horford's consistency continued even in the second half of the season. On February 25, he would have 22 points, 13 rebounds, seven assists, and two blocks against the Golden State Warriors in a win. Four days later, in a loss to the Nuggets, he had 21 points, 16 rebounds, and 4 assists. In his first game of March, he then had 31 points, 16 rebounds, and two steals when the Hawks defeated the Bulls.

Despite being in a good position to secure one of the top spots in the Eastern Conference, the Atlanta Hawks would stumble in the final few games of the season not long after their star centre was able to put up good numbers on a four-game winning streak. After that winning stretch, the Hawks would end the season losing six games in a row and were in bad shape heading into the playoffs.

Despite the inconsistencies surrounding the Atlanta Hawks, Al Horford remained the sole consistent force in the roster. He would finish the season with 15.3 points, 9.3 rebounds, and 3.5 assists. Among all the centres that season, Horford was the best regarding making plays for others. With his 55% field goal shooting, Al was also fifth in the league in that department while also finishing 11th concerning rebounding. For total efficiency, Horford just fell one slot below the top 15 as he was growing to be ever more efficient in all the facets of the game. Because of that, Horford was named the centre of the All-NBA Third Team that season.

The fifth-seeded Atlanta Hawks, who finished the season with a 44-38 record, headed into the playoffs to face off against the Orlando Magic, the team that swept them out of the second round of the last postseason. The highlight of the matchup was, of course, the head-to-head battle between the two best centres in the Eastern Conference. Al Horford would have his chance to exact revenge on Dwight Howard, who dominated him throughout the 2010 playoffs.

In Game 1, the Hawks would throw a bevy of big men on the dominating Dwight Howard, who finished the game with 46 points and 19 rebounds. Though Howard was doing a lot better than Horford in that game, Al still got the win while contributing 16 points and six rebounds. The Magic would get the better of the Hawks in Game 2 with their centre still outplaying Atlanta's best big man. Horford would finish with 10 points and ten rebounds while Howard had 33 points and 19 rebounds.

The Atlanta Hawks had done their part in stealing a home game away from the Magic. All they had to do now was to secure their home floor all /2hroughout the series to proceed to the second round. But Al still struggled against the dominant centre, who had 21 points and 15 rebounds. Horford would only have 13 points and seven rebounds, but the rest of the Hawks stood up to take the win. In another fierce battle in Game 4, the Hawks would triumph while the two giants in the middle battle each other for double-double performances.

Heading to Orlando for Game 5, the Atlanta Hawks had all the confidence in the world while riding a 3-1 lead. But the Magic would deflate that confidence by dominating them in a blowout game. Not willing to go to Game 7, Atlanta would beat the Magic in Game 6, though Horford did not have his best scoring performance. He would have 10 points, 12 rebounds, and six assists in that closeout game. And though he was again thoroughly outplayed by Howard in the matchup, Horford's team came out with the important wins to secure a third consecutive second round appearance.

Versus the top-seeded Bulls in the second round, Horford would meet his old Florida Gators partner in the paint Joakim Noah on the other end of the bleachers as he anchored the Chicago defence just as well as Al did for the Hawks. The defensive tenacity between the two centres was palpable as neither of them had good scoring nights. But Al Horford did every other thing right when he finished the game with 13 rebounds, 4 assists, and 2 blocks for the Hawks, who won an upset in Game 1.

But, coming into Games 2 and 3, Al Horford was unable to solve the physical and swarming defence of the Chicago Bulls. He might have rebounded, defended, and facilitated well for the Hawks, but he would only combine for 16 points in those two losses. However, he would have his best game of that year's playoffs when he finished Game 4 with 20 points and a win to boot. In that game, Al Horford made 9 of his 11 shots while playing a little above 30 minutes only.

But the Chicago Bulls would dig deep into their defensive strategy to frustrate the Atlanta Hawks anew in Games 5 and 6 and to proceed to the Eastern Conference Finals for a chance at an NBA Finals slot. Al would combine for only 19 points in those two losses. Overall, he did not have the best playoff outing that year after averaging only 11.3 points, 9.6 rebounds, and 3.5 assists. After scoring on 55% of his shots during the regular season, Horford was limited to 42% during the playoffs.

The Injury Season

The NBA would enter a labour dispute lockout shortly after the 2011 Finals ended. As a result, players were not allowed to practice with their teams and no franchise was able to make any offseason moves to improve their roster. Even players had to resort to playing in other leagues and working out on their own to keep themselves in shape. Al Horford, on his part, would participate in several international tournaments as a member of his Dominican Republic basketball team while the NBA was still hammering out a new labour agreement.

The regular season would only start late in December, and with teams relying on a short training camp, players were either sluggish or out of shape. Horford was not an exception as he struggled out of the gates for the Atlanta Hawks. Al was neither scoring in bunches nor was he rebounding possessions like he used to in the early moments of that season. His scoring high for the first ten games was only 16 while his best rebounding performance was when he grabbed 11.

As if sluggishness was not the only problem Al Horford and the Hawks had to worry about, their luck just got worse. In the first quarter of their game against the Indiana Pacers on January 11, 2012, Horford would tear his left pectoral muscle and would not return in the match. Initial findings ruled him out to miss about three to four months of action after he underwent surgery to have his torn muscle fixed.

In that unfortunate 2011-12 season for Al Horford, he would average only 12.4 points and seven rebounds in 11 games of action. Horford would only have two double-double games that season as he barely had any impact for the Hawks in his appearances.

The Atlanta Hawks would make the fifth seed in the Eastern Conference after winning 40 of their 66 games even without their starting centre. They would meet the Boston Celtics in the opening round of the playoffs and would even with Game 1. However, they would end up losing Games 2 and 3 to the veteran squad. Trying to get a boost from their frontcourt, the Atlanta Hawks would activate Al Horford in Game 4 after the centre missed nearly four months of action due to injury. He scored 12 points in his first game back since January 11, but his Hawks would end up losing again. Atlanta fell 1-3 in the series.

In Game 5, Al Horford did not look like he missed significant playing time and seemed like a fresh player on the floor in front of the Atlanta faithful. Horford would power the Hawks to a victory in Game 5 and inched closer to the series deficit. Al finished the game with 19 points, 11 rebounds, three assists, three steals, and three blocks to make it look like as if he was not injured for the majority of the regular season. But despite another valiant effort from him in Game 6, the Celtics ended up winning the series. Horford had 15 points, nine rebounds, and four assists in Game 6 as his 14-game season abruptly ended.

Return to Form, Career Bests

The great showing from Al Horford during the 2012 playoffs in limited action was a testament to the work he put in during the extended absence he had to take because of the torn pectoral muscle. He would take that with him to the next season and soar higher than he ever did. With Joe Johnson moving on to another team that season, Horford was going to be the primary source of offense for the Hawks. He did not disappoint.

Right out of the gate, Al Horford performed his best as the primary option on the Hawks' offense. After dropping a good outing in their first game, Al would explode for 23 points and 12 rebounds in a victory over the Oklahoma City Thunder in their second game. Al then had 16 points, nine rebounds, and three blocks in the match after that.

Another one of Al Horford's first dominant performances was when he had 20 points and ten rebounds against the Sacramento Kings. He would outplay DeMarcus Cousins on both ends of the floor in that win. Then, on November 21, Al Horford nearly had first triple-double and was a rebound shy away from his first one. With Horford playing the role of facilitator, he ended the win with ten assists on top of the 15 points and nine rebounds he had. Two days after that, he had 26 points, 13 rebounds, and 3 blocks in a win over the Charlotte Bobcats.

Late in November until early December, Horford would mount seven straight double-double performances while also collecting several assists per game in the process. His ability to play both ends of the floor while making timely passes to teammates led to five wins for the Hawks over those seven games. Al was quickly and undeniably becoming one of the brightest centres in the game at that point in time.

Then, in back-to-back wins against the Chicago Bulls and Detroit Pistons, who both had capable big men guarding the paint, Horford delivered 21 points and ten rebounds per game in those victories. Despite a loss on the final day of 2012, Horford did have 18 points, 13 rebounds, and four assists versus the Houston Rockets and their bruising defensive centre Omer Asik.

Al Horford opened the year 2013 with a good start by posting 20 points in a win against the New Orleans Hornets. After that, he had 18 points and 15 rebounds in a one-point loss to the Detroit Pistons. The Hawks, after that, would face a slump as they won only one game out of the next seven. In breaking that slump against the new-look Brooklyn Nets, Al Horford would deliver 17 points and 13 rebounds.

On January 21, 2013, Horford would improve his season high to 28 points when he hit 12 out of 20 field goal attempts in the Hawks' win over the Minnesota Timberwolves. He also had ten rebounds, two steals, and three blocks in that game. In his next game, he solidified a win against the Boston Celtics by providing 24 points, 13 rebounds, and 2 steals in two overtime periods.

The Atlanta Hawks may have lost against the New York Knicks in their game on January 30, but their centre did have a good night by hitting all eight of his shots to score 16 points. Then, in the Hawks' next game, Horford would go for 22 points, ten rebounds, six assists, and three blocks for another well-rounded stat line. One would say that, with the numbers that Al Horford was putting up while leading the Atlanta Hawks to another possible playoff appearance, he would be named as an All-Star for the third time in his career.

However, Al Horford would not see his name as a reserve for the Eastern Conference All-Star team despite putting numbers he has never put up in his career. He was one of the notable snubs as the voting format had eliminated the centre position and replaced it with "frontcourt players" to adjust to ever-changing NBA game that has seen fewer centres dominating the paint while smaller forwards excelled at keeping up with the quickening pace. A bevy of better performing frontcourt players aside from the legitimate centres had rightfully earned their slot in the All-Star team over Al Horford.[3]

With averages of 15.6 points, 9.8 rebounds, and 3.3 assists when the All-Star reserves were announced, Al Horford would make known his claim as a forgotten star by putting up 21 points and ten rebounds in a win over the Dallas Mavericks on February 11. In the next game, he would go for 26 points, 12 rebounds, five assists, and two steals in another victory for the supposed-to-be All-Star centre. And while the Hawks may have lost to the powerhouse Miami Heat team right after the All-Star break, Horford dominated the small frontline by providing 27 points on 12 out of 15 shooting together with nine rebounds. Since those three games, Al Horford would mount together nine consecutive games of scoring above 20 points.

Horford had a lot of notable performances during that incredible personal run for himself. He would have 24 points, eight rebounds, and six assists in a win against Sacramento on February 22. Then, he was responsible for beating the Milwaukee Bucks with his 23 points, 11 rebounds, three assists, two steals, and two blocks. After that win, he would go to Detroit to deliver another solid career performance. Posting 23 points and 22 rebounds on the Pistons, Horford went for his first 20-20 game of the season on February 25. But he was not done with career nights, because two days later, he had a new high of 34 points to go along with the 15 rebounds, three assists, and five blocks he collected in a win against the Utah Jazz. After those games, no one could deny the fact that Horford was indeed the biggest snub of the All-Star team.

After his great run had ended, Al Horford proceeded with the rest of the season by posting 13 double-double outings over the course of the last 19 games that he played to end the season. Among the notable performances he had in that final run was when he had 26 points and 15 rebounds in a win over the Bucks on March 20. A week after that, he had 26 points and 12 rebounds in a win in Toronto. Finally, he would beat Milwaukee in his last game of the season on April 12 by posting 18 points, 17 rebounds, and six assists.

At the conclusion of the regular season games, Al Horford averaged career highs in points and rebounds. He normed 17.4 points and 10.2 rebounds in addition to 3.2 assists, 1.1 steals, and 1.1 blocks. On top of that, Al was shooting an incredible 54% from the floor as the Atlanta Hawks' go to guy on offense. He would also finish the season with a career best 43 double-double performances. But again, he would get snubbed as he was not named an All-NBA player. Nevertheless, he led the Hawks to a 44-38 regular season finish and the sixth spot in the Eastern Conference playoff picture.

Al Horford and the Atlanta Hawks would go up against an Indiana Pacers team that dominated the rest of the Eastern Conference during the regular season. However, the Hawks could not stand up against the suffocating defence of the Pacers and were left with a loss in Game 1. Matching up against the bigger Roy Hibbert, Horford had 14 points and six rebounds Game 2 was the same story. Al Horford could not score against the inside defence of the Pacers and was left shooting jumpers from the perimeter, though he made those shots on a regular basis. Nevertheless, the Hawks lacked the dominant performance they needed from their centre, who only finished that loss with 13 points and ten rebounds, though he did have five assists.

Back in Atlanta for the next two games, Al Horford and his Hawks seemed to have solved the Pacers' unbeatable defence. They would anchor their offense on Al Horford, who was too mobile for Roy Hibbert and was too big for the backup centres of Indiana. He would finish that blowout win with 26 points, 16 rebounds, two steals, and two blocks. And in what seemed like an easy win for the Pacers, Horford outplayed his defenders again and would only log in 30 minutes to put on 18 points, five rebounds, and four assists in another big win.

Unfortunately for the Atlanta Hawks, the Indiana Pacers were too good of a championship contending team to lose one more game. The Pacers would dominate the Hawks in Game 5 while winning Game 6 in a defensive approach. Horford had 14 points and nine rebounds in Game 5 but was outplayed by Hibbert in Game 6 as the Atlanta Hawks failed to reach the second round for a second consecutive year.

While the Atlanta Hawks may have underperformed during the regular season, it was clear that they were a team built for the playoffs considering how hard they battled against a much better Indiana Pacers team. And for Horford's part, his future as a centrepiece on offense was getting brighter considering the numbers he put up as the Hawks' best player despite getting snubbed in the All-Star voting. Those kinds of performances from both Horford and his Hawks could only mean that they were going to get better in time.

Another Injury Season

Banking on the performances he had during the regular season last season, Al Horford would come into the following season with renewed vigour and with more hunger as the best player on an Atlanta Hawks team that featured new faces in the likes of Paul Millsap and DeMarre Carol, who would both contribute well for the Hawks. But the biggest change they made was replacing Larry Drew with former Spurs assistant Mike Budenholzer. Budenholzer would instill the same kind of passing and ball movement used by the Spurs to make the Hawks a more potent and fluid offensive team.

With his eyes set on a better season and a return to the All-Star Game, Horford would star the season posting big double-double games and great scoring performances. In his second game of the season in a win against the Toronto Raptors, he would have 22 points and 16 rebounds. After that, he had 16 rebounds again in a losing effort to the LA Lakers before beating the Sacramento Kings with his 27 points and ten rebounds. He even made his one and only three-point attempt in that game as he kept on extending his range deeper outside the perimeter.

Midway through November, Al Horford would score at least 20 or more points in three consecutive games. He had 24 against the Charlotte Bobcats when he made 9 of his 15 shots. After that win, he had 23 in their loss to the New York Knicks before going for 20 points on 8 out of 15 shooting in a win versus the Philadelphia 76ers. From then on, Al Horford was rarely seen scoring under double digits as the Atlanta Hawks always found a way to go to their versatile centre with their ball movement whether it was inside the paint, down at the low post, or within the perimeter.

For his fourth double-double game of the season, Al Horford would go for 17 points, 11 rebounds, and three assists in a win over the Detroit Pistons on November 22. A week later, he had another double-double when he posted 17 points and 12 rebounds when the Hawks defeated the Dallas Mavericks. Then, on December 4, he would have 21 points on 8 out of 17 shooting in a win against the LA Clippers before winning a game against Cleveland by scoring 22 points. After that match, his double-digit scoring stretch would end in a loss to the Oklahoma City Thunder. That was the only time he scored under 10 points that season.

Three days after that loss to the Oklahoma City Thunder, Al Horford would tie his career high in points by posting 34 points on 15 out of 23 shooting together with 15 rebounds and two steals in a win against the Washington Wizards and their bruising frontline players. From that point on, Al Horford was on a tear on both ends of the floor as he was displaying his dominance in all facets of the game.

Such instances of Horford's ability to control the game at every facet was the back-to-back all-around performances he had against the Lakers and the Kings in the middle of December. Versus LA, he had 19 points, 11 rebounds, and five assists. And then, when he met up with Sacramento's DeMarcus Cousins, he outplayed the talented centre by putting up 25 points, ten rebounds, five assists, and four blocks in a battle of two great big men.

After that win against the Kings, Horford would shoot 11 out of 15 in only 22 minutes of action against the Jazz in a blowout win. He had 23 points that game. He would then round up four consecutive games of scoring 20 points or above by going for 21 points and 11 rebounds in a narrow loss to the Miami Heat and then 25 points and eight boards in a win versus the Cleveland Cavaliers on December 26. However, that would be the final game that Horford would play for the Hawks that season.

In that double-overtime win against the Cavs, Horford would stretch his right arm up during an inbound play with about two minutes left in the first overtime period. That stretch would spell his doom that season as he would immediately halt playing. Al would exit the game after a timeout and would not return to play that night or any night that season for that matter.[4]

Al Horford was diagnosed with a completely torn right pectoral muscle after tearing the left one two seasons before. It was first diagnosed as a bruised right shoulder, but it turned out to be worse than they thought. After surgery, Al was ruled out of the remainder of the season and would even miss the playoffs. The Hawks badly needed him as they went 22-31 in the next 53 games that their centre missed. The need was direr when they were beaten by the Pacers again in the first round of the playoffs.

The injury at the end of what was going to be another productive season for Al Horford was ever more disappointing considering that he was on pace to set a new high on the scoring end. In the 29 games that he played, Horford averaged 18.6 points on a high of 56.7% shooting from the field. He also posted at least 20 points 13 times while failing to score in double digits only one time that season. Horford also had nine double-doubles that season, which would have been his return to the All-Star Game after two seasons of missing it.

Return to All-Star Glory, Dominating the East, Conference Finals Appearance

Al Horford would make a full recovery just in time to join the Atlanta Hawks in training camp to prepare for what was going to be one of the best seasons in franchise history. After a full year under the tutelage of Budenholzer, the Hawks would take their ball movement to greater heights by utilizing the strengths of their players. Both Horford and Millsap were good passers for big men and could both stretch the floor with their outside shooting. Horford was also a great option at the post, especially during plays when their movement was not going to work. In addition to that, the roster was full of shooters ready to spot up from beyond the arc whenever the ball would find them. It was going to be a beautifully formed team that would make the rest of the East tremble.

In his eighth NBA season and at 28 years of age, Horford was still in his prime and ready to lead the Hawks in that upstart season. However, considering that Budenholzer wanted to preserve his best players and get them as far as possible from injuries, Horford's minutes were thoroughly decreased that season. However, his production and efficiency would not fall far from what he and the world were used to seeing from the Dominican Republic native.

In the Hawks' first win of the season, Horford would only play 28 minutes but had 20 points on 9 out of 14 shooting from the field. Though it was in a loss to the Spurs in their third game of the season, he did have a good all-around game with 10 points, seven rebounds, and six assists. After that, he posted 24 points, ten rebounds, and three steals against the Charlotte Hornets on November 7.

After dropping three of their first four games, the Atlanta Hawks suddenly won 12 of their next 16 outings thanks to their efficient ball movement and suffocating defence. While Horford's offense was not quite as great as the production he put up the past two seasons, he was still able to make do with what he could do while playing fewer minutes. He was the Hawks' anchor on the defensive end of the floor and was also facilitating well for his teammates.

Despite the decreased minutes, Horford was still able to contribute on the scoring end in a lot of ways. On November 14, he would have 19 points on 8 out of 10 shooting in only 28 minutes of action against the Miami Heat. Though it was in a losing effort against the Toronto Raptors, he would have 23 points, nine rebounds, and four assists while shooting 11 out of 16 from the floor in only 32 minutes. Then, in only 18 minutes when the Hawks blew the Hornets out early, Al had 11 points on 5 out of 6 shooting. And on December 8, Horford tallied 25 points, eight rebounds, three assists, and three blocks in only 30 minutes when the Hawks defeated the Indiana Pacers.

Though the Atlanta Hawks were winning at a record pace, Al Horford was still apparently adjusting to the system after he missed the majority of last season. Nevertheless, he would find his groove as December went on to post numbers similar to the career pace he had the previous two seasons. On game in point was when he delivered 21 markers, ten rebounds, and six dimes in 33 minutes in a win over the Chicago Bulls on December 15. After that, he had 20 points on more than 70% shooting from the field in a blowout win against the heavily favoured Cleveland Cavaliers. And at the tail end of the Hawks five-game winning run, Al had 20 points over the defensive specialist DeAndre Jordan of the LA Clippers. In his final game for the year 2014, Horford would have 20 points in a win against the Milwaukee Bucks. Because of performances like those in December, he would earn a player of the week award for that month.

The New Year was just as good to both Al Horford and the Atlanta Hawks as they continued what was going to be a 19-game winning streak for the team. They were unbeaten for the whole month of January, which saw memorable performances from the consistent Al Horford, who was even better that month. With the way he was leading the Hawks while putting on good performances, Horford was on track to make a return to the midseason classic.

After consistently finding himself in the low double-digits of scoring in January, Horford would go for 19 points, 16 rebounds, and four assists in a win over the Denver Nuggets. Then, on January 13, Horford would culminate a fantastic all-around performance with a triple-double game—the first of his career. He had 21 points, ten rebounds, and ten assists in only 29 minutes of action in that win against the Sixers. He would then hit all eight of his shots in his next game, which was against the Raptors. Al had 22 points, five rebounds, and five assists in only 28 minutes.

Continuing the winning streak, Horford would provide solid numbers all month long. He had 22 points, nine rebounds, and four assists in Chicago on January 17. Six days later, he went for a double-double of 14 points and 12 rebounds together with three assists and three blocks. Then on January 25, he made 8 of his nine attempts to go for an efficiently put 19 points before beating the Brooklyn Nets with his 20 points, ten rebounds, and five assists. In the final outing of that 19-game winning run, Al Horford contributed with 23 points, 11 rebounds, four assists, and three blocks.

Though the winning streak may have ended, it put the Atlanta Hawks at a good solid first place in the Eastern Conference, and they would hold on to that spot for the rest of the season. Horford, while leading the Hawks to a great season, would go for numbers worthy of All-Stardom. In his first game after the streak ended, Al had 21 points and 13 rebounds in a win over the Wizards. And in a battle between the two best teams that of the regular season, Horford had 12 points, 14 rebounds, and six assists in 28 minutes of action when his team bested the Golden State Warriors. And heading into the All-Star break, Horford would combine for 50 points and 20 rebounds in the two games before the midseason classic.

Just as suspected, Al Horford made his return to the All-Star Game that season due in large part to the reliable efficient numbers he was putting up despite playing fewer minutes while leading the Hawks to a great regular season standing. Speaking of the Hawks, Horford was not alone coming into the midseason classic. He was joined by teammates Jeff Teague, Paul Millsap, and Kyle Korver, who were all putting up solid outputs that season in Atlanta's fantastic winning pace. That was the first time since 2011 when a single team had four All-Stars in a season. The last to do it were the Boston Celtics.

Horford's solid performances would not end after his return to the All-Star Game. On February 27, he would make 7 of his nine shots to score 17 points together with 13 rebounds and four assists while barely playing 31 minutes in a win over the Orlando Magic. Then, against the Cleveland Cavaliers on March 6, he had 19 points, nine rebounds, and six assists in a win against a fellow powerhouse. Nine days after, he would show up in Los Angeles to go for 21 points and five steals in a win.

With the Atlanta Hawks at a steady pace to secure home court throughout the postseason, Horford's minutes would soon see a decrease as the playoffs were nearing. He would only contribute a single double-double in the final stretches of the season while scoring above 20 points only twice more after that game in LA. Horford would average 15.2 points, 7.2 rebounds, 3.2 assists, and 1.3 blocks while only playing a career-low 30.5 minutes. He was the model of efficiency all season long.

With the Hawks winning 60 games and securing the top seed in the Eastern Conference that season, everyone thought that their first round matchup against the Brooklyn Nets would be a piece of cake. And with Horford being the better of the two centres that would clash in the series, his dominance over Brook Lopez was almost a sure-fire probability.

The Hawks would open the series by winning two straight games on their home court while their star centre had double-doubles. Horford's best outing in those wins was when he put up 14 points, 13 rebounds, and seven assists in Game 2. But Al would suddenly see a struggle in Game 3 after shooting only 25% all game long in a loss to the Nets. Brooklyn would then surprisingly tie the series up though Horford had 17 points.

Not willing to let the upstart Brooklyn Nets take the series lead, Al Horford went into Game 5 to put on one of his best games during the postseason. He would have 20 points, 15 rebounds, five assists, two steals, and two blocks at the end of that win. Then, in Game 6, he would only play 31 minutes while contributing 18 points and seven rebounds when the Atlanta Hawks finally dispatched the gritty team in an easy win.

The Washington Wizards, their second round opponents, were a different story. Armed with a bruising frontline of Nene and Marcin Gortat, Al Horford was going to prepare himself for bumps at the conclusion of the season. Against the imposing and physical frontline, he would struggle to shoot only 37% in Game 1, which the Hawks surprisingly lost. However, he had 17 points, 17 rebounds, and seven assists that game. But with their home court advantage on the line, Al would provide 18 points and six assists in a win in Game 2.

Despite failing to secure home court advantage again in a loss in Game 3, Horford would have another solid performance of 18 points and ten rebounds in a win in Game 4 to tie the series up. Then, in Game 5 in Atlanta, the centre would go for 23 points, 11 rebounds, and five blocks as he controlled the game on both ends of the floor in that win. Finally, in the closeout game, he did his best to eliminate the Wizards and proceed to the Eastern Conference Finals for the first time in his career by providing 13 points on 6 out of 9 shooting.

Heading into the Conference Finals, the Atlanta Hawks were the favourites to make it to the NBA Finals after they had dominated the Cleveland Cavaliers in the regular season. But the playoffs were a different story. Horford and the rest of his All-Star teammates struggled against the tough defence of the Cavs and had no go-to guy to provide them points whenever they needed to. Al was a good option on offense, but his scoring was predicated on proper positioning and ball movement instead of one-on-one plays, which the Atlanta Hawks needed whenever the Cavs frustrated their flow and fluidity.

In the end, Atlanta would fall in a four-game sweep after the Cleveland Cavaliers exposed their weakness—they had no alpha male. It was a team that had good players that made the All-Star team by playing unselfishly. Even their centre was passing the ball a lot. However, they sorely needed a go-to-guy. Al Horford, in the past two seasons, was that guy. But in Budenholzer's system, he was an essential gear in a rampaging vehicle. Disrupt one gear, and the whole machine falls apart. That was what happened in that series. No Hawks player, including Al Horford, was able to perform well versus the Cavs and it spelled doom for their hopes of making the Finals that season.

Final Year in Atlanta

After that sorry loss to the Cleveland Cavaliers in the 2016 Eastern Conference Finals, the Atlanta Hawks were coming into the 2016-17 season with the same core of players that made the All-Star team. For the better part of the early season, they would even show the same hunger that made them the top-seeded team in the East a season prior after winning seven of their first eight games.

In those eight games, the centre in the middle was just as good for the Hawks as one of their vital pieces on both offense and defence. In the team's second game of the season, he would have 21 points, nine rebounds, and three blocks in a win in New York. He followed that up with 18 points when the Hawks defeated the Hornets and then had his first double-double game of 16 points and 12 rebounds against the very same team. Horford would then beat the Miami Heat with his 17 points and 13 rebounds on November 3 before going to their game against Brooklyn to put up 21 points, eight rebounds, and four assists. He would punctuate a good start to the season by going for 26 points and eight rebounds while shooting 11 out of 15 from the floor in the Hawks' win against the New Orleans Pelicans. The highlight of that performance was how far Al Horford had gone in terms of his shooting. He would make a career-best four three-pointers in that game as Horford continued to evolve and adjust to the changing NBA game that has come to favour the three-point shot heavily.

As the season progressed, the Atlanta Hawks suddenly struggled with consistency as some of their core players underperformed in certain stretches while the team's defence was not as tenacious as it was the previous year. Horford himself was beginning to battle inconsistency as he saw stretches of low-scoring outputs despite his consistent rebounding and defensive presence. Nevertheless, he would have one of his best games early on when he had 21 points and 13 rebounds against the OKC Thunder, a Western powerhouse, in a win on November 30.

Al Horford would then continue a career-best 23 straight games of scoring at least 10 points leading into December. He had his 23rd consecutive game of double-digit scoring when he scored 14 points in a win over the Dallas Mavericks on December 9. His streak ended at the hands of the Thunder when he only had 9 points on December 10 in a loss.

Horford and the Hawks would bring their inconsistencies to December as the team would lose four of their first seven games that month while their centre would not explode for a terrific game until the 18th day when he had 21 points and ten rebounds in a win over the Boston Celtics. But the team would then end the year right by winning seven of their final eight games of 2015. Horford had a then-season best of 30 points to go along with 14 rebounds in his last game of that month in a win in Houston.

It would not take long for Al Horford to eclipse his season high. On January 9, 2016, he would have 33 points, ten rebounds, six assists, and four blocks in a phenomenal outing against the Chicago Bulls. From then on, inconsistent performances started to pile up again. There were stretches when Al would go for good nights on a statistical basis while he would float on other nights. The Hawks were just the same considering that they were simply trading winning stretches with mini losing skids as the season unfolded.

Despite the inconsistencies on both the personal and team levels, Horford solidified his fourth All-Star appearance by going for about 19 points and 4 assists in the last four games before the midseason break. After joining three other Hawks All-Stars the previous year, only Al Horford and Paul Millsap made it that season for Atlanta. However, Horford nearly got snubbed again as he was only a replacement All-Star for the injured Chris Bosh. But an All-Star appearance is still an All-Star appearance.

Following the break, the Hawks would lose their first three games of the second half of the season. This time, Horford's inconsistencies could not be faulted considering he was doing better in those games. In one of those outings, which was in a loss to the historic 2015-16 Golden State Warriors team, Horford had 23 points, 16 rebounds, six assists, three steals, and five blocks in one of the best-rounded efforts one could get from a centre in the NBA. Horford would then help snap the skid by scoring 18 points on 8 out of 11 shooting from the field against the Bulls. Then, in a win against the Hornets, he had another beautiful stat line of 13 points, 16 rebounds, and six assists.

As the season was nearing its end, the Atlanta Hawks suddenly found their bearing and got back to their winning ways. They would win 15 of their final 21 games of the season while Horford scored at least 20 points in four of those games. He also had five double-doubles in the same stretch of games for the Atlanta Hawks, who qualified for the fourth seed with their record of 48 wins against 34 losses.

At the conclusion of the season, Al Horford averaged similar numbers from that of the previous season. He normed 15.2 points, 7.3 rebounds, 3.2 assists, and 1.5 blocks. Though the figures were the same on paper, Horford's game had apparently evolved to adjust to the new style of basketball. The biggest change that Al was clearly trying to do in his game that season was his three-point shooting.

In the past eight seasons, Al barely took three-pointers though he was making the ones he was shooting. But, during the 2015-16 season, he was more than willing to take the long shots and was making 34% of them. That's an impressive number for a centre. And, for that matter, he had made a total of 88 three-pointers after 256 attempts that season as compared to the combined total of 21 makes on 65 attempts in the past eight years. That goes to show how much Al Horford was working on his outside shot in the offseason and how much more confident he had gotten in terms of attempting those kinds of long balls.

In the first round of the postseason against the young Boston Celtics, Al Horford immediately made his presence known by posting 24 points, 12 rebounds, and two blocks in a Game 1 victory. He then added 17 points and five blocks when his team won Game 2 by a large margin as they were hoping for another deep playoff run that season.

But two setbacks in Boston forced the Atlanta Hawks to a stalemate with their upstart foes. Though Al had 8 points, 13 rebounds, six assists, two steals, and four blocks in Game 3, it was clearly his scoring that the Hawks needed the most after losing by eight. He was again struggling to put points up on the board in Game 4 as the Hawks fell to the Celtics in another game.

With the series tied two wins apiece, the Hawks relied on solid team play to grab series control once again with a 27-point win in Game 5. Al Horford, in only 24 minutes of action, had 6 points, eight rebounds, and four assists in his third consecutive struggle from the field. But when things got important, he scored 15 points in Game 6 to help his team eliminate the Celtics and to proceed to the second round.

But much like the past year's playoffs, the Cleveland Cavaliers owned and exposed the Atlanta Hawks to make them look lost on offense while their superstar opponents dismantled them on the defensive end. After losing Games 1 to 3 by double digits, it was a foregone conclusion that their season was about to end. Game 4 was tightly contested, but the Cavs ended up winning it to sweep Atlanta once again. Horford averaged about 15 points in that series, but it was his rebounding that was missed. He only averaged 3.5 rebounds in those four games.

Little did everyone know that Al Horford had already played his final game for the Atlanta Hawks after being their most consistent two-way player since getting drafted back in 2007. By the end of the regular season, he was set to become an unrestricted free agent that could sign with any team that wished for his services. As good centres were a rarity in the NBA at that era, Horford was going to be one of the most sought-after players in free agency during the offseason.

Signing with the Celtics, First Season in Boston

At 30 years old, Al Horford was still in the prime of his career, though his production was soon going to face a decline. However, Horford's game was predicated more on skill instead of athleticism, and that fact alone would help him play at an All-Star level for a lot more seasons to come. Moreover, his skill level at the centre position was invaluable for any team considering his services because of how well he could fit with just about any system.

The biggest contenders to securing Al Horford's services were, of course, the Atlanta Hawks, who offered him about $106 million over the course of the next five seasons. However, Horford was also mulling over the $113 million four-year contract that the Boston Celtics offered him. In the end, while it was not a purely financial decision, the four-time All-Star centre decided to move to Boston to become a Celtic.[5]

Several rumours pointed out to why Al Horford decided to leave the Atlanta Hawks, the team he called home for nine seasons since 2007. Some say it was because the Hawks were not willing to shell out more money for him. But others would say that it was because the Atlanta Hawks had already committed to sign centre Dwight Howard to a long-term contract. Horford, being the alpha centre since 2007, was rumoured to be uncomfortable sharing space and minutes with Howard. Though rumours and reports all pointed out that Horford never liked Howard, he would, however, dispel those rumours and would instead point to the reasons why he joined the Celtics instead of the reasons why he left the Hawks.[6]

Al Horford would say that he joined the Celtics because he loved the fans there. Horford also stated that he always admired Celtics head coach Brad Stevens and even said he had a good relationship with him. Stevens, in his short tenure with the Celtics, was all about the substance and skill of his players rather than flash and highlight reels. That was what Horford was always about.

Another thing to note was that Horford was joining a team that was always about the winning tradition. The Celtics have a long history of winning titles and games as evidenced by their 18 championship banners hanging up from the rafters of their home court. And at that point of the roster's life, the Celtics were on the verge of making a breakthrough and were one great free agent signing away from contending for a title. Al Horford was that All-Star acquisition the Celtics needed, and he was on his way to pairing up with an upstart young point guard Isaiah Thomas, who made the All-Star team a season prior despite standing only 5'9".

Though he was still adjusting to new teammates, a new coach, and a new system, Al Horford fit in well for the Celtics after scoring in double digits in his first three games while making sure he was impacting outcomes on all facets of basketball. He had 11 points, five rebounds, six assists, and four blocks in only 27 minutes in his Celtics debut. It was in a win against the Nets. Then, he had 11 points, seven rebounds, and five assists in a close fight in Chicago before going for 14 points in a win over the Hornets.

Horford, however, would miss the next nine games for the Celtics because of a concussion he suffered during one of the team's practices. Since the NBA was strict regarding its concussion protocols, Al had to miss extended time until such a day that he would progress well with the injury and make sure he was at his best state to play a physical basketball game.

Al would make his return on November 21 in a win over the Detroit Pistons. Without showing any signs of concussion or rust, he broke out by putting up 18 points, 11 rebounds, five assists, two steals, and three blocks while matching up Andre Drummond, who was quickly gaining recognition as the best centre in the East. Against the young and talented Karl-Anthony Towns of the Minnesota Timberwolves in his next game, he had 20 points, six rebounds, five assists, and three blocks. Proving he was what the Celtics needed to go to the next level, he had 17 points, five rebounds, and eight assists in the team's third consecutive win since Horford came back to the line-up. His best game of the young 2016-17 season was on December 2 when he had 26 points, eight rebounds, two steals, and six blocks in a win against the Sacramento Kings.

Al Horford is currently averaging All-Star worthy numbers of 14.9 points, 6.5 rebounds, 4.6 assists, and 2.7 blocks. He is on pace to breaking his career best in assists and blocks while making sure he is an integral part of a rising Boston Celtics squad especially with the good relationships he has formed with the coach and the players, notably Isaiah Thomas and Amir Johnson.

CHAPTER 4: INTERNATIONAL CAREER

As the best player in Dominican Republic basketball history and as the most important part of a growing basketball culture in that part of the world, Al Horford has participated in several international competitions as his country's primary weapon against the other powerhouses in the FIBA Americas tournament.

Horford first participated in international competition during the 2009 FIBA Americas Championship wherein he averaged 14 points, 10.2 rebounds, and 2.8 assists per game. The Dominican Republic, however, was not yet up to the challenge of the other powerhouses in that region and would not qualify for the FIBA World Cup.

Al Horford then played with his country in the same event in 2011 and has grown to become a better and more dominant centre on the international stage. He averaged 19 points, 9.2 rebounds, and 3.1 assists all tournament long as his team made significant improvements but still failed to qualify. And in the 2012 Olympic Qualifying Tournament, he normed 18 points, 9.4 rebounds, and 3.2 assists despite the fact that the Dominican Republic failed to qualify again. But with Horford on the team, the Dominican Republic had made significant strides over the past years and is only going to get better as basketball becomes a bigger sport in that country.

CHAPTER 5: PERSONAL LIFE

Al Horford's father, Tito Horford, was the first player in Dominican Republic history to make it to the NBA. Though he did not have a very fruitful career in the big league, Tito sowed the fruits that would later become a family of good basketball players led by his eldest son, Al. Al's mother, Arelis Reynoso works as a journalist.

Al Horford is not the only man in the family with a good basketball pedigree. His brother, Jon Horford, also stands 6'10" and played college basketball in Michigan and Florida, which is Al's alma mater. Jon, who is five years younger than Al, plays for the Canton Charge in the NBA's Developmental League after he once played and dominated in the Liga Nacional de Baloncesto in the Dominican Republic.

Al's youngest brother, Josh, is merely a young high school senior over at Grand Ledge, where the two older Horfords graduated from. He currently stands a little over 6'6" and averaged 11.3 points, 6.1 rebounds, and 1.5 blocks in his senior year as a forward in Grand Ledge. He is expected to try and follow his brother's dreams of making it to the NBA despite not being as dominant as Al was in high school. Al Horford, aside from Jon and Josh, has two sisters namely Maria and Anna.

On December 23, 2011, Al Horford married 2003 Miss Universe Amelia Vega, a native of the Dominican Republic. At the age of 18, Vega was the youngest Miss Universe winner since 1994 and has since tried her hand at becoming a recording artist and entrepreneur. She and Al had their first child together on February 23, 2015. Their son is named Ean Horford. They had their second child on November 28, 2016. Until now, January 2021, they have four children together.

CHAPTER 6: IMPACT, LEGACY, AND FUTURE

No matter how you look at it, the one thing that stands out about Al Horford is his consistency. Ever since he joined the NBA in 2007, he has always been a consistent force on both ends of the court. He scores and defends at a good rate throughout the ten years he has played in the NBA, so much so that there are almost no signs of slowing down for him. And for the nine seasons he played with the Atlanta Hawks, he was always their most valuable player because of his offensive and defensive consistency.

What makes Al Horford a consistent player is the physical attributes he possesses coupled with the skill level that he has. At 6'10" and about 250 pounds, he has size and strength to play against bigger centres. He is also athletic enough and quite mobile for his size to the point that he could keep up with faster forwards while making sure he rotates quickly to the weak side on defence to alter or block shots. That is the reason why he was always a valuable defender for any team he has ever played while also contributing big time on offense.

Speaking of offense, only a few players come to mind when talking about the level of skill that Al Horford possesses on the offensive end. He could bully and dominate at the post using his size and strength. He is mobile enough to put the ball on the floor and attack the basket. He has the basketball IQ to know when and where to position himself for drop passes and easy baskets. And he has a soft touch from the perimeter all the way to the three-point line to stretch defences and keep his man honest when defending him.

But the one thing that stands out about Al Horford's offensive skills is his passing ability. He has always been one of the best passing centres in the NBA, and such a talent has helped him become an All-Star in several different systems under different coaches. Such skills have made him the model of consistency all through these years while former All-Star centres he has played against like Dwight Howard, Roy Hibbert, and Andrew Bynum have all fallen off in terms of production. Those players have fallen off because they rely solely on size and athleticism and because of their failure to adjust to the evolving NBA game.

Speaking of adapting to the changing game, Al Horford is one of the few centres today that could fit in just about any era of NBA basketball because he could do damage from anywhere on the floor. While formerly restricting himself to making inside shots and hitting timely midrange jumpers, Al Horford has extended his range all the way out to the three-point line to become a deadly marksman for a centre. This was done in response to the league's growing reliance on the three-point line as big men have come to shoot more from that distance these past few years.

Names such as DeMarcus Cousins, Karl-Anthony Towns, and Kristaps Porzingis all come to mind when talking about centres that fit right into the new style of NBA basketball because of their versatility on offense. But, in comparison, Al Horford has long been more consistent than any other versatile centre on the planet considering all the All-Star and playoff appearances he has had while making sure he was also impacting the game from a defensive standpoint.

A few years from now when 7-footers and other centres dominate both the inside and outside games of basketball, one would point to Al Horford as one of the pioneers of such a style of play considering that he has always been that type of player ever since he came into the league in 2007. Horford's legacy and impact on the game will be determined by how much he has helped changed the way it is played and how much he has adjusted his style to suit the needs of the evolving sport of basketball. And considering the way he has been playing while other centres have been following suit, Al's future in today's NBA is a bright one, even as he ages because of how well he has adapted his skills to change and how such an adaptation has made all the teams he has played for contenders.

More Information

Career statistics

Legend						
GP	Games played	GS	Games started	MPG	Minutes per game
FG%	**Field goal** percentage	3P%	**3-point field goal** percentage	FT%	**Free throw** percentage
RPG	**Rebounds** per game	APG	**Assists** per game	SPG	**Steals** per game
BPG	**Blocks** per game	PPG	**Points** per game	**Bold**	Career high

NBA
Regular season

Year	Team	GP	GS	MPG	FG%	3P%	FT%	RPG	APG	SPG	BPG	PPG
2007–08	Atlanta	81	77	31.4	.499	.000	.731	9.7	1.5	.7	.9	10.1
2008–09	Atlanta	67	67	33.5	.525	.000	.727	9.3	2.4	.8	1.4	11.5
2009–10	Atlanta	81	81	35.1	.551	**1.000**	.789	9.9	2.3	.7	1.1	14.2
2010–11	Atlanta	77	77	35.1	.557	.500	.798	9.3	3.5	.8	1.0	15.3
2011–12	Atlanta	11	11	31.6	.553	.000	.733	7.0	2.2	.9	1.3	12.4

Year	Team	GP	GS	MPG	FG%	3P%	FT%	RPG	APG	SPG	BPG	PPG
2012–13	Atlanta	74	74	**37.2**	.543	.500	.644	**10.2**	3.2	**1.1**	1.1	17.4
2013–14	Atlanta	29	29	33.1	**.567**	.364	.682	8.4	2.6	.9	**1.5**	**18.6**
2014–15	Atlanta	76	76	30.5	.538	.306	.759	7.2	3.2	.9	1.3	15.2
2015–16	Atlanta	**82**	**82**	32.1	.505	.344	.798	7.3	3.2	.8	**1.5**	15.2
2016–17	Boston	68	68	32.3	.473	.355	.800	6.8	**5.0**	.8	1.3	14.0
2017–18	Boston	72	72	31.6	.489	.429	.783	7.4	4.7	.6	1.1	12.9
2018–19	Boston	68	68	29.0	.535	.360	**.821**	6.7	4.2	.9	1.3	13.6
2019–20	Philadelphia	67	61	30.2	.450	.350	.763	6.8	4.0	.8	.9	11.9
2020–21	Oklahoma City	28	28	27.9	.450	.368	.818	6.7	3.4	.9	.9	14.2
Career		881	871	32.5	.517	.364	.755	8.2	3.3	.8	1.2	13.9
All-Star		5	0	12.0	.667	.200	1.000	4.4	1.6	.4	.4	6.2

Playoffs

Year	Team	GP	GS	MPG	FG%	3P%	FT%	RPG	APG	SPG	BPG	PPG
2008	Atlanta	7	7	**39.6**	.472	—	.741	**10.4**	3.6	.4	1.0	12.6
2009	Atlanta	9	9	28.0	.424	.000	.667	5.8	2.0	.7	.7	6.9
2010	Atlanta	11	11	35.3	.523	1.000	.839	9.0	1.8	.7	1.7	14.6
2011	Atlanta	12	12	39.0	.423	.000	.769	9.6	3.5	.4	1.0	11.3
2012	Atlanta	3	2	36.0	**.588**	—	.750	8.3	2.7	**1.3**	1.3	15.3
2013	Atlanta	6	6	36.3	.494	—	.667	8.8	3.0	1.0	.8	**16.7**
2015	Atlanta	16	16	32.6	.507	.222	.750	8.6	3.7	.8	1.4	14.4
2016	Atlanta	10	10	32.7	.466	.393	**.938**	6.5	3.0	1.2	**2.4**	13.4
2017	Boston	18	18	33.9	.584	.519	.759	6.6	**5.4**	.8	.8	15.1
2018	Boston	**19**	**19**	35.7	.544	.349	.827	8.3	3.3	1.0	1.2	15.7
2019	Boston	9	9	34.4	.418	.409	.833	9.0	4.4	.4	.8	13.9
2020	Philadelphia	4	3	32.0	.480	.000	.571	7.3	2.3	.3	1.3	7.0

Year	Team	GP	GS	MPG	FG%	3P%	FT%	RPG	APG	SPG	BPG	PPG
	Career	124	122	34.6	.501	.402	.778	8.1	3.5	.8	1.2	13.6

College

Year	Team	GP	GS	MPG	FG%	3P%	FT%	RPG	APG	SPG	BPG	PPG
2004–05	Florida	32	25	22.8	.480	—	.582	6.5	.9	.8	1.6	5.6
2005–06	Florida	39	39	25.9	**.608**	.000	.611	7.6	2.0	**1.0**	1.7	11.3
2006–07	Florida	38	36	**27.8**	**.608**	.000	**.644**	9.5	2.2	.7	**1.8**	**13.2**
	Career	109	100	25.7	.586	.000	.619	7.9	1.7	.9	1.7	10.3

International statistics

Year	Competition	GP	GS	MPG	FG%	3P%	FT%	RPG	APG	SPG	BPG	PPG
2008	FIBA Centrobasket	5	5	31.8	.662	.500	.750	9.8	2.2	.4	1.4	14.4
2009	FIBA Americas Championship	8	8	33.1	.534	.000	.692	10.2	2.8	1.1	1.0	14.0
2011	FIBA Americas Championship	10	10	33.3	.514	.250	.811	9.2	3.1	1.9	1.0	19.0
2012	FIBA Centrobasket	5	5	34.2	.483	.455	.605	10.0	3.2	.2	2.4	17.2
2012	Olympic Qualifying Tournament	5	5	31.8	.500	.000	.688	9.4	3.2	.6	.4	18.0

REFERENCES

Notes

[1]
"Arelis Reynoso Es Una Madre Y Abuela de NBA". Diario Libre. 12 May 2015. Web

[2]
"Al Horford". NBADraft. Web

[3]
Zimmerman, Kevin. "NBA All-Star 2013 Snubs: Stephen Curry, Brook Lopez Among Biggest Absences". SB Nation. 24 January 2013. Web

[4]
Golliver, Ben. "Hawks" Al Horford Officially Out for the Season". Sports Illustrated. 1 January 2014. Web

[5]
Weitzman, Yaron. "Al Horford, Celtics Agree to $113 Million Contract, Per Report". SB Nation. 2 July 2016. Web

[6]
Pandian, Ananth. "Al Horford Says He Didn't Leave Hawks Because of Dwight Howard Signing". CBS Sports. 13 July 2016. Web

Made in the USA
Columbia, SC
09 December 2024